zly in

rt (Bob)

zly in

rt (Bob)

SEASONS OF THE GRIZZLY

IN KNIGHT INLET

Library and Archives Canada Cataloguing in Publication

Scriba, Robert, 1952-
    Seasons of the Grizzly in Knight Inlet / Robert (Bob) Scriba.

ISBN 978-0-919537-77-4

    1. Grizzly bear--British Columbia--Knight Inlet. 2. Grizzly
bear--Food--British Columbia--Knight Inlet. 3. Salmon--British
Columbia--Knight Inlet. I. Title.

QL737.C27S372 2008   599.784'15309711   C2008-905697-3
Printed in China

Book design by Natasha Duff, Kask Graphics Ltd.
Campbell River, British Columbia, Canada
www.kaskgraphics.com

Photography by the author

SEASONS OF THE GRIZZLY

IN KNIGHT INLET

INTRODUCTION

Throughout my life growing up on a small grain farm in northern Alberta, as a logger, hunter and outdoorsman, bears were mistrusted, feared and hunted. These were only black bears, but to our way of thinking a bear is a bear. Over the years I observed bears in many different habitats and situations. I have rousted out their dens while hunting and logging. I have thrown rocks at cubs up a tree while their mom paced back and forth in the forest; I have shot them when they wandered through my space. I am not proud of these actions in my past, but have moved on to respect and admire these beautiful and magnificent salad eating carnivores.

A few years ago while tree planting in Alberta, I chased a couple sub adult grizzly cubs with a school bus full of cheering co-workers down an old logging road for a couple hundred yards before they veered off into the bush. I had to stop a little farther to let the crew off to plant trees. Down an angle cutline tore momma bear, straight towards us as we loaded our trees. She was roaring and spitting her displeasure, scraping up grass and dirt and spinning loops as she warned us to mind our manners as we worked in her territory. Needless to say, we were on our best behavior for the rest of that day.

On another occasion a friend of mine and I lounged in front of our beautiful alpine camp above Cecilia Lake on the headwaters of the South Kakwa River in western Alberta. The horses grazed on the rich meadow grass, their bells adding to the peace and harmony of the scene in front of us. Half a mile away was a Coyote teasing a large grizzly bear as it dug for marmots. My friend looked over and said 'we could be there in ten minutes if we worked those horses to a lather!' I don't know what he had in mind as the bear disappeared over the ridge. Ten minutes later that bear came tearing over the very ridge we would have been at if we had 'lathered them up!'

A few years later, Fay and I with good friends, watched a mom grizzly with cub foraging in the high alpine of Horn Ridge above Kakwa Falls, also in western Alberta. Another grizzly bear seemed to stay with them, albeit, at a respectful distance of about a hundred yards. It was one of those beautiful afternoons where the light and air is crystal clear with a light breeze to keep the bugs at bay. The fall colors were at their most brilliant, the marmots were whistling their frantic warnings and the bears were packing on their hibernation fat. Their fur, glistened at every step or gust of wind, had that gorgeous shimmering, grizzled, sheen that gives them their name. I remember that setting as if awakening refreshed to new aspirations, vowing to change and learn to appreciate the wonders of God's creation.

I am still amazed everyday by the great bears. They are not the predatory monsters portrayed by the hunting magazines I used to subscribe to. Instead, I have observed a gentle giant who really just wants to be left alone to wander and the freedom to take its place as one of the great carnivores on this earth.

Glendale River Reflection.

I have just witnessed one of Mother Nature's major
miracles and it is the life cycle of the pink salmon and the
wildlife that depend on them. From the time the salmon's
eggs are laid in September and October to when they
emerge in March and April, to their long journey from
their birthing spot in the river to the Pacific Ocean up
to Alaska, half way to Japan and then all the way back to
their river of birth eighteen months later, they are
running a gauntlet of predators who want to eat them.
When they leave their rivers of birth, they are about
one inch long and it takes about 3 pink salmon to
weigh one gram.

Some unknown instinct tells them to swim down river,
through Knight Inlet to the ocean miles away, eating and
being eaten by predators all the way. How do they know
where to go to find the rich nutrients they need to grow
so quickly? When they come back to their river of birth
eighteen months later, they will weigh from four to seven
pounds. What drives them to such single minded
purpose to run a continuous gauntlet of predators for
about eighteen to twenty months, just to come home
to their birthplace and to begin once again the miracle
of life, only to die within a few days? They are already
starting to rot and deteriorate while making a last valiant
effort to make it to the spawning ground.

GLENDALE RIVER

A salmon may be one of the few species born in this world who knows, if nobody eats it during its life, when it is going to die, within a month or so. How would you live if you knew that eighteen months from now you are going to die?

A holding pool in the Glendale spawning channel

Even once dead, the pink salmon continue to benefit the world they have left. Their rotting remains in the river will feed all the microscopic life in the river and estuaries. The bottom of the food chain thrives on these rotting carcasses.

The eagles, gulls and bears drag their caught salmon up into the forest to eat. The left over remains release their nutrients to the forest ecosystem very slowly but beneficially. The scat from the birds and animals gets spread over the forest floor, acting as a very valuable fertilizer for all the plants of the forest. The nutrients from this, loose animal scat, composed of salmon, is a highly dissolvable fertilizer, readily utilized by the forest.

It has been shown that up to seventy percent of the nitrogen in the mosses, ferns, berry bushes and trees, is derived from salmon carried as far as one hundred and fifty meters from the rivers by the bears, birds and other fish eating animals.

Pacific Pink Salmon

Pacific Pink
Salmon Pinks, humpbacks
Oncorhynchus gorbuscha

Distribution and Harvesting

Wild pink salmon is the most abundant of all Pacific salmon species. In North America, pinks are found as far south as Puget Sound, in Washington state and as far north as the Mackenzie River, in the Yukon Territory. In Asia, they are found as far north as the Lena River in Siberia and as far south as southern Japan. Pinks are also plentiful in the Sea of Okhotsk which is fished by China, Russia, Japan and other nations. Pink salmon live only two years and have a relatively simple life cycle. Of all salmon, except chums, pinks spend the least time in fresh water, drifting downstream to the sea as soon as they emerge from the rivers gravel. They are also the smallest and shortest lived of all Pacific species with a life span of just two years. As a result, their migration pattern is the least wide-ranging, keeping them close to shore for the two years they spend in the ocean. Adults leave the ocean in the late summer and fall and usually spawn in streams a short distance from the sea. Males on the spawning grounds develop an extremely humped back (giving all pinks the market name of "humpback") and both sexes change colour from bright silver to pale gray on the back with a white to yellowish belly.

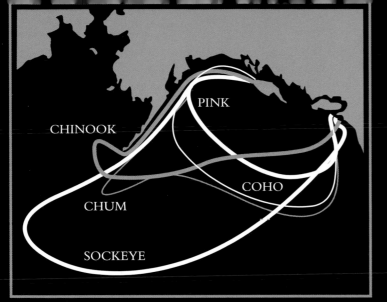

CHINOOK

PINK

COHO

CHUM

SOCKEYE

Habits and History of Salmon

There are seven species of North American Pacific salmon: Chinook, chum, coho, cutthroat, pink, steelhead and sockeye. Although each species has a unique appearance and different habits, they share many characteristics. They are anadromous meaning their eggs are laid and hatch in freshwater and their young spend at least some of their early lives in freshwater before swimming to the sea to grow and mature. Their ability to find their way home again when it is time to reproduce is one of the most remarkable things about salmon. In fact, salmon have been known to travel thousands of kilometers in the ocean, as well as battle strong river currents and waterfalls to reach their hatching place. Pacific salmon, with the exception of cutthroat and steelhead, spawn only once and die within days of digging their nests or 'redds' in the gravel and mating. Their bodies float down rivers and decompose, filling the water with nutrients for other species of animals and plants. Live and dead salmon are also important food for birds like eagles and gulls and mammals such as bears and otters. In this way, salmon contribute to the health of freshwater ecosystems.

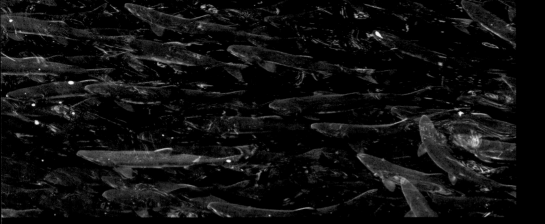

Salmon lay their eggs in nests or 'redds' that the females dig in the gravels of streams or in some cases lakeshores. The gravel must be free of silt and well oxygenated. Young salmon require cold, clean, well-oxygenated water. They are very sensitive to any activities like forestry and farming. Other human activities like building roads and cities, can damage or destroy freshwater salmon habitats if they are not carried out in an environmentally friendly manner.

Salmon have existed for millions of years. They provided food for First Nations living along the coast and interior of British Columbia for thousands of years. Since the late 1800s, salmon have supported a vibrant commercial fishing industry, vital to the establishment and well being of many coastal communities. Sport fishing for salmon is also a popular recreational activity for local citizens as well as visitors. In addition to having different spawning habits, each species has a unique appearance and life history.

It is an awesome sight to see thousands of pink salmon holding in every tannin stained pool along the river. They are waiting for their time to ripen and spawn. The stench of thousands of dead and rotting fish wafts down the river and out over the estuary on the prevailing breezes, calling the predators and scavengers to the Glendale smorgasbord. Eagles, gulls, seals and bears come from miles around for this annual reunion and buffet.

It doesn't take much to disturb the peace of the waiting pool; it can be an eagle flying over-head or just a frisky fish protesting its impending fate. Shortly after the survivors of the gauntlet have spawned and died, the Glendale area quiets down as winter descends. In March the great pink salmon cycle starts all over as the eggs emerge from the gravel to begin the next journey.

The salmon are known as a 'keystone' species. This means that they are an essential species to the overall health and benefit to the environment around us. Without the salmon there would be a lot fewer animals and the forest would not be as healthy as it is. About one hundred and thirty different mammals, birds, fish and of course humans use salmon as part of their diets. The salmon populations have been steadily declining for the past several years. We all have various ideas why this is happening, depending on one's point of view or how this decline affects one's lifestyle. It is easy to point fingers at the warming climate, over fishing by commercial or sport fishers, the loggers, the fish farms, the seals or a myriad of other problems the salmon struggle through everyday of their short lives. Everybody one talks to has an opinion about how to fix the problem. Generally the answer is to shut down one industry or the other, or being as drastic as shooting the seals. Most people understand there is a problem and have opinions about how to fix it. Caught in the middle of these various interest groups are the government agencies responsible for the industries and the protection of the salmon and the environment in which we all live. The Department of Fisheries and Oceans, or 'D.F.O', is responsible for the well being of the salmon. This organization has many dedicated people who live and work in the communities affected by the loss of salmon.

'KEYSTONE' SPECIES

These professional people struggle with decreased budgets, low manpower, and huge areas of land and water to manage. Scientific studies to enable our governments to have accurate facts and figures requires cooperative efforts between concerned companies, interest groups and the manpower of the D.F.O. Knight Inlet Lodge employs three people to assist the D.F.O. by monitoring two fish traps along the Glendale River and spawning channel. The first trap is at the spawning channel weir. The entire pink salmon population born in the spawning channel has to cross the weir on their way to the ocean. It is quite easy to funnel all the pink salmon fry through the trap. The fry splitter trap is designed to catch approximately five percent of the fry swimming through here. It is a simple mathematical calculation to then determine how many fry are leaving the channel to begin their hazardous journey to the ocean.

know the Glendale River produced about 10.8 million fry. I think that more than 15 million fry leaving the Glendale system are very positive numbers. I am looking forward to the return of these fish in the late summer of 2009 to see how many survive the long and dangerous journey back. Three to four percent are supposed to survive to spawn so we need about 525,000 adult fish to return next year for all to be normal and sustainable.

In August another monitoring station will be installed where the RST is now. It is an electronic beam that shoots across the river. It shows every salmon that swims upstream to spawn and by comparing the numbers from year to year we can start to see what is going on in our area. Since a healthy number of salmon fry leave the Glendale in the spring we can say the river is healthy and we've done our part in assisting the continued viability of the pink salmon here. If the predicted numbers don't return next fall, further studies will be required beyond our river to find out why. Scientists continue to study the effects of fish farms, sea lice, ocean warming, sea salinity, sea acidification, pollution, logging practices, fishing quotas, by-catches and a myriad of other problems that may contribute to the decline of the wild salmon stocks up and down the west coast of North America. Governments of countries, states and provinces are continually monitoring and updating catch quotas and treaties in various zones of the Pacific Ocean. These studies assist the governments to make good policies to protect the salmon while also protecting the jobs, vitality and diversity of the west coast.

Throughout the months of March and April the pink salmon have been emerging from their birthing gravels and floating down the river toward the ocean to begin their journey. At the same time another miracle is also taking place in the mountains and valleys overlooking the Glendale River. In April the bears come out of hibernation. After almost six months of sleeping, giving birth and fasting, it can be challenging for the bears to find food right away. Avalanche chutes and low elevation wetlands and estuaries provide the first food sources. New growth on the grass and sedge flats, berry bushes and roots, get them started.

Shellfish along inter-tidal zones and any carrion found provide the nourishment needed to rejuvenate their bodies after a long winter. The bears have lost about a third of their body weight and they are shedding their heavy winter coat of fur.

Late May & June is breeding time

for the bears. This is the time of year the big males are most aggressive. They may attack and kill cubs; they will pursue female bears relentlessly while waiting for estrus and mating time. They will compete vigorously with other males for the right to breed a female. They can be severely wounded in combat with rivals and may not survive these encounters.

The females are about 5 or 6 years old when first breed. They can have multiple mates and have cubs sired by different males. Boars can also sire many litters with different sows.

The females are bred now but have delayed implantation. A sow only becomes pregnant in late October if her body has sufficient fat reserves to carry her and her cubs through hibernation. The cubs, ranging from one to four, are born in late January or February. They are only about one pound and are hairless, blind and toothless. It is easier on the female to nurse a baby than to continue a pregnancy while she is fasting. Her milk is very rich in nutrients, so the baby bears do not require as much as other large mammals. They nurse to gain weight and strength so they are strong enough to follow their mother when she leaves the den.

Throughout their young lives, the cubs are never far from mom. They are underfoot, underbelly or shadowing her every action. Sometimes she will hide them nearby in the forest or they will be playing with a sibling, climbing a tree or mauling an imaginary foe stick. Any squawk of alarm from the cub will bring instant action from mom. This is one situation that we as wilderness wanderers want to be careful of. Make sure the bears know we are around.

The parenting sow is a very strict disciplinarian. She expects her cubs to obey her commands immediately. When she says something, it can mean the difference between life and death. No whining is allowed in the bear world.

It is the sole responsibility of the female bear to raise the cubs. She accepts this daunting job of feeding, protecting and teaching her young family everything they need to know in order to survive in this dangerous wilderness. It is a tough world out here, even for bears. Only about one half the cubs born survive the first year. Cubs die of starvation, or of not being strong enough to follow mom when they leave the den. Other bears may kill them, and there are often accidents.

Bears have large brains, are very intelligent and have very good memories, so they are very teachable. Mom has to show the cubs where to find food, shelter and safety.

Bears are very curious and will explore everything around them. They use all their senses to determine if something is good to eat or not. The cubs also have to gain a lot of fat to be able to survive the coming winter. It is a lot of fun to watch the young cubs mimic their mom as she finds food throughout the summer. Remember, they learn to do by doing.

Watch as the cub tries to roll a rock over on the beach to get at the succulent morsels underneath. He pulls and tugs with both front feet and all the power his small body can muster to slurp up the shore crabs, gunnels, isopods or any thing else he finds edible before it wiggles away. I always wonder if they ever accidentally roll a rock over onto their back foot, and would they then do the sore toe hop

DEVILS CLUB

Watch as they try to pull an elderberry bush down to where they can pull off a few of the bright red berries. Bears add to the vegetation by eating the berries and spreading their seeds throughout the forest, and giving the seeds a good place to germinate in the scat pile.

A GRIZZLY WE NAMED
PRINCESS

Who can't help but be amused, watching a grizzly we named Princess sitting on her rock, waiting for mom to catch a fish, so she can saunter over to get her share. Princess acts as a lookout for mom as she slurps salmon eggs off the bottom of the river. She might look bored, but she is learning by watching all the action around her. She notices all the other bears, their body language and how the hierarchy of the bear world works. She knows that without the protection of her mom, she could not be in the best fishing hole on the river. The sea gulls, the eagles, crows, ravens and mallard ducks tread water nearby, arguing and squawking over any bits or morsels dropped or stirred up by the feeding bears.

Even the older cubs, protected by their aggressive mother, could not be here without her. One of these female cubs is showing the same bold behavior as her mom. Hopefully, she will survive long enough to raise her own litter. Next year will be a different story for them, once they are making their own living. Doesn't this sound familiar? The comparisons between the human world and the animal world can be quite similar.

Spruce Bud

This is a time of relative peace and quiet around the Glendale. The weather is generally sunny and warm, and the winds are calm. The river is running low and clear, and the foliage on the trees and bushes is the most intense greens of the mature leaves before they start to change color for the fall season. Most of the elderberries, devils club, pacific crabapple and the other wild berries are ripe and showing off their brilliant tasty fruit. We see the Columbia black-tailed deer grazing on the shore. The fawns are starting to lose their protective spots. The buck's antlers are almost fully grown and still encased in the soft velvet covering.

PEACE AND
QUIET

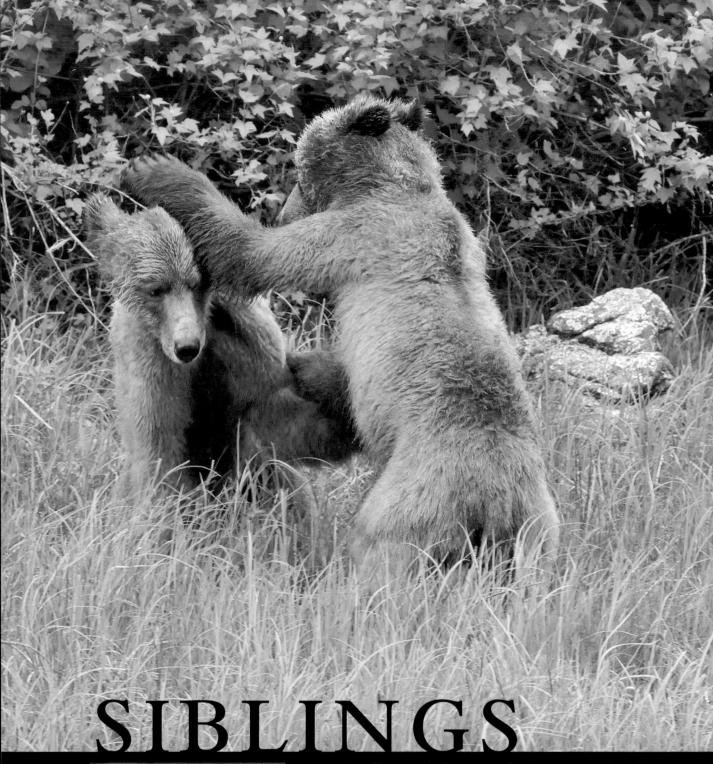

SIBLINGS

The cubs will stay with their mom for about two and a half years. In late May of their third year, mom chases them away to make their own living. She will then be bred to start the cycle all over. The siblings will stay together for another couple of years or until one of them becomes sexually mature. It is great fun to watch these young bears experience their first year away from their mom. They are not unlike our own children; some bold, some meek, some workers and some more laid back.

July is feeding time on the estuary sedges and in the berry patch. The sedges are very high in protein, up to twenty five percent. Bears also roll rocks over in the intertidal zone to eat rock crabs, barnacles, mussels and isopods. The berry patch provides a wide buffet for bears in the Glendale area. Salmon berry, devils club, huckleberry, thimbleberry and elderberry are the most common choices. There are of course many more. As the bears start to congregate on the estuary their personal space or safety zone starts to become smaller.

They are aware of each other but tolerant. The moms with cubs are very vigilant and the sub-adults are very cautious about how close any other bears can come. Even black tail deer chase these kids away. The bears seem to recognize their position in the hierarchy of the bear world, so not too many confrontations happen. Body language tells vigilant observers all the information they need to determine anybody's intentions.

THIMBLE BERRY

The end of July and early August is a time of varied diet for the bears of the Glendale estuary. The sedges are more mature, so now less palatable, but the berries have been ripening just in time. The thimbleberries with their sweet aroma have matured, tempting the bears up into the bush.

The huckleberries are turning bright red and deep blue and the elderberries are showing off with large, bright red mouthfuls of juicy decadence. It is a time for the bears to wander up high in the forest looking for a variety of different foods. Now is when they may dig up a squirrel, or its stash of cones. They may find a log full of high protein ants and grubs or just the right patch of devils club berries to eat.

They will wander down to the beach at low tide to roll rocks over and slurp up the squiggly critters they find hiding underneath. Shore crabs, isopods. Gunnels and even starfish are edible. This is a time of peace and calm in anticipation of the frenzy soon to descend upon the river. Where are the salmon?

Elderberry

BRIGHTRED
MOUTHFULLS OF
JUICY DECADENCE

The northern harrier hawk glides over the flat unsuspecting meal while the eagle sits regally on its favorite perch overlooking its kingdom.

The surviving merganser chicks are almost as large as their mom and the belted kingfishers are busy teaching their youngsters to fish.

The black bears are wandering back and forth, as the tide dictates, from the beach to the berry patch. They too are searching for the variety of berries and protein needed to gain weight as the summer progresses. You shudder at the sounds of their teeth scraping the barnacles off the rocks and the crunch of the shells of mussels as they are greedily scraped and chewed up. You have to wonder how long their teeth last at this dining style and pace. You have to be happy that you don't have to clean up after them when you see the drool running out of the corners of their mouths.

As the tide slowly rises the black bear disappears silently into the protective canopy of the forest, his path marked by the occasional disappearance of a berry bush as he pulls it down to slurp a mouthful of mixed berries and leaves. Soon the bush snaps back into place and you would never realize that any bear could be within your area. Oh! what was that flash of brown that just dove into the water? Wait a few seconds to see if it was your imagination: no, there it is; a mink. This fur bearing member of the weasel family is very much at home in the water, like his cousin, the river otter. We see these little hunters of fish and small game often, as they scurry along the beach rocks, snooping in every nook and cranny looking for any meat to eat.

River Otter Mink

GLIDING SILENTLY, SWOOPING DOWN

Before you know it, mid August rolls around. Subtle changes are happening in the Glendale River and estuary. There is a new odor in the air: the smell of autumn. The seemingly calm waters belie the dramas unfolding, out of sight beneath the reflective surface. As the tide ebbs, the large mud bank is exposed to our view. The receding waters also reveal a new crop of food to watchful predators. A fish, stranded in a shallow pool, splashes around in a vain attempt to escape back to the deeper protective waters of the river. All it is managing to do is to attract the attentions of a myriad of predators, waiting patiently for just such a helpless victim. Here come the first gulls and crows, squawking and cawing, announcing to the world that lunch is served. The bald eagle leaves her roost a quarter mile away, gliding silently, swooping down, scattering the noisy throng in panic.

Grabbing the floundering fish in her razor sharp talons, with a mighty effort of a couple of powerful heaves of her six foot wingspan, she lifts the three pound salmon clear of the water and muscles her way to a safe perch for her meal. The noisy mob can do little but complain over the loss of their lunch, and finally disperse to find something more manageable to eat.

There seem to be more actors in the impending drama. The seals are starting to be more noticeable in the estuary. And aren't there more eagles hanging around? And more gulls, more great blue herons; isn't that a new bear over there? What are they all hanging around for? A trip up the river soon reveals the hidden secrets. Look sharp. Isn't that a school of pinks over there? Good news spreads quickly over the air waves; the salmon are back.

They are sitting in the pool under the overhanging tree. They are in the river mouth. There is a flurry of activity under the boat as we motor quietly up river on the rising tide. Soon we are as far up as we can go, and we shut the motor off. Silently, we drift back downstream. The only sound to break the peace is the whisper of eagle wings over head or a splash of water as a seal grabs a salmon for its next meal. Gulls are arguing in the distance as the little boat quietly displaces the reflections on the surface of the river. There sits another eagle on the leaning tree, just past the island. Another splash is heard just around the bend downstream. Expectantly we wait as the ebb tide and the river flow carry us quietly toward that mysterious splash. There is a barely audible gasp as one of the guests spots the splashee, a lone bear trying to catch a fish in water too deep. He is now standing on the bank, looking for another chance. He suddenly notices us drifting closer and closer. He is unsure whether to run or not. We pause to let him make up his mind.

Another flutter of water in front of him attracts his thoughts back to fishing. Once again the fish escapes and the bear turns downstream beside the river toward the sedge flat. He is in no hurry. The river widens out here and we give him a wide berth as we float past. He watches us out of the corner of his eye, knowing we mean him no harm. He is a new bear to us, but, undoubtedly he was here last year for the salmon feast. An afternoon like this is remarkable to most of us in this boat. We left the lodge a couple hours ago, not knowing what we may see, but full of anticipation. The blue skies, or rainy skies if that's what it is, the mountains, the river, the wildlife and the silence is what we all need. Even if for only a few minutes, we some how heighten our senses and become attuned to what is happening around us. What an honor it is to experience nature at her best.

Through late July and August the bears have been wandering up and down the length of the estuary and river. They are looking for anything to eat. At low tide they are down on the beach rolling barnacle encrusted rocks over, gathering any squiggling protein hidden beneath. As the tide floods the beach, they disappear into the privacy of the forest. Here, they are searching for any berries they may have missed on earlier picking trips. Their keen noses also direct them to a freshly buried cache of cones and mushrooms the squirrels have stored away for the coming winter. After rooting through this stash, they may roam higher up the mountain searching for a patch of berries ripening later in the season due to the higher elevation. On the way up the bear rips open a rotten log, slurping up the ants and grubs scurrying to escape this late season disaster to their home.

Their insatiable appetite drives the grizzly and black bear to continuously wander, searching for the next morsel. The late summer is a time for the female bears to wander, all the while leading her cubs through her territory. She is constantly showing them where and how to find food, shelter and safety. This is a constant time of danger and learning for the youngsters. The cubs also do a lot of play fighting and wrestling with each other and their mom. This is not only fun but teaches them how to handle themselves against more serious foes later in life. They must know how to look after themselves by the time they are about two and a half years old when mom will tell them 'you're on your own!' As the summer progresses, any bear family is beginning to encounter more and more bears in the Glendale river basin. Their territory and personal space seems to be shrinking. Bears from many miles around are beginning to gather here for the impending salmon feast they are expecting. This will be the high volume, high fat and protein source needed for all the bears. This is the only way these bears have to gain the weight needed in time to go into hibernation in good enough shape to survive the next six months of fasting.

As the bear family makes its way back down to the river on familiar paths, they stop to leave their mark on one of the sign posts scattered throughout the forest. They also check out who else may be in the area. A good sniff on the ground and tree scar tells a very informative story. Who is in the area? What is their mood? Are they male or female? If nothing else, a good back rub feels sooo good!

The end of August is here and September brings with her the first signs of autumn. The first changes, from green to a hint of yellow and red and orange and brown are showing up in the forest and along the river. The sun does not seem to be as warm as its arc in the sky lessens. There are new odors on the wind, spreading out over the estuary, the inlet and beyond the mountains.

THEY STOP TO LEAVE THEIR MARK

Each pool in the river is filling more everyday with pink salmon. They lie here, waiting for their eggs to ripen, seemingly reluctant to continue the final leg of their life journey. They are driven by the same unknown instinct that took them from this river a year and a half ago down the inlet and out into the Pacific Ocean and back. What drives these fish from the relatively protected deep water of these pools up into the shallow riffles, past the gaping jaws and sharp claws of waiting bears to the spot they were born at to spawn and fertilize their eggs, only to die a few days later? Life, the greater good and survival of the species, can be the only answer. These fish do not have the same motivations as their human counterparts. I asked the question many times last season of our guests: ' would you leave the ocean to go into the river if you knew that your body would become misshapen or you could get eaten by a bear, just to lay your eggs and die in a few days?' Good for the bears, forest, eagles and all of Mother Nature, the fish have been programmed to sacrifice their lives and are now in the river. Let their struggle to spawn continue.

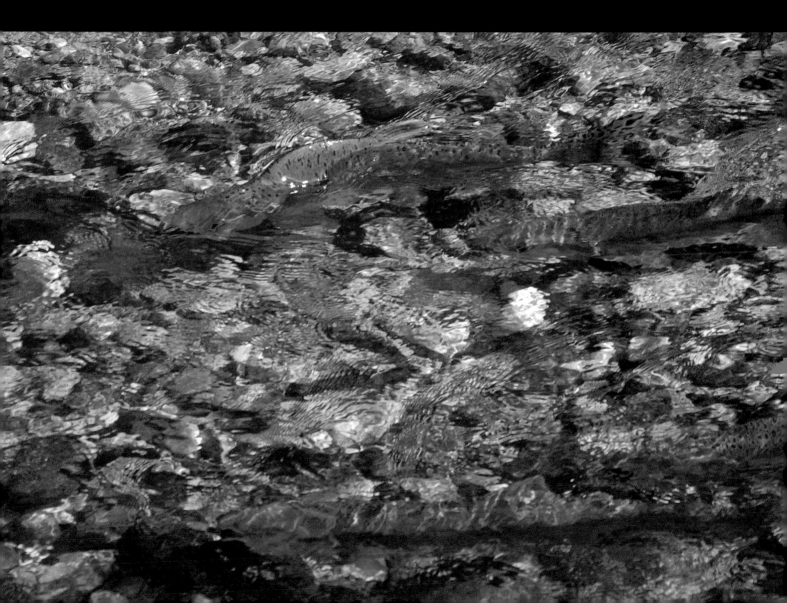

T h e   s a l m o n   h a v e   l e f t   t h e   i n l e t   and turned into the Glendale estuary only to be met by a horde of harbor seals. These raiders of the deep are also motivated by the easy pickings of the confined spaces in the shallow waters of the cove and mouth of the river. The large numbers of fish in such a small area allow the seals to expend minimal energy to catch their next meal. Often, all we see is a sudden wake on the surface of the water as the seal chases down its prey, then, a sudden splash when it catches it. The successful seal then plays, catlike, with his hapless victim as it devours it. A couple sea gulls circle overhead to collect any remains the seal may leave behind.

The salmon need to get past the first riffle in the river to escape the threat of the seals. Around the first bend in the river, beside the island is that gravel barrier. Here is where the first grizzly bear gauntlet begins. Unlike the seals, the bears prefer to fish in shallow water. The fish are much faster than a bear in any deeper water. In the shallow water of the riffle the fish are slowed down as they struggle and splash their way toward the next pool ten or twenty feet away.

Their valiant efforts alert the waiting bear who quickly pursues his next meal. The older bears make quick work of this pursuit as practice makes perfect. The younger bears expend no end of energy in reckless splashing, jumping, diving, swatting and biting at these slippery elusive calories. Just when they think they have a fish trapped under their paw, it gives a last wiggle and escapes. It can be a very entertaining comedy of errors to watch. Often, you can see the frustration in the look of disbelief on their face. The young bear also gets confused by the riches of the river. He will be in hot pursuit of one fish when another splash beside him distracts his attention momentarily, and he will lose both fish. I have seen him plop down in the middle of the river, looking around furtively to see if anyone saw his antics, he re-evaluates his techniques. Soon he is motivated by another fish struggling toward him, so up he gets to try once again.

PRACTICE MAKES PERFECT

Most of the fish make it past this first obstacle only to have the tide flood in, covering that bar and allowing the seals to once again have another chance at these same fish for another three or four hours before the tide ebbs. They have to make it past one more riffle before the tidewater no longer affects the river.

Just around the next bend in the river is a fish counter. It has been installed by the Department of Fisheries and Oceans. There is an electronic beam through which every returning fish has to pass to get any further upstream. This beam tells a computer as each fish passes and leaves an imprint on the hard-drive. This computer is monitored daily by a Knight Inlet Lodge staff member. Every once in a while a grizzly bear has to investigate what is going on in his territory. Equipment gets turned over, torn down, climbed upon and tasted or chewed on to make sure it is in full compliance with the bear world. Every once in a while a bear has to go sit in the river in front of the beam to make sure it is well counted as well.

The next decision for the returnees is caused by the scent from two different water sources combining at the fork. The water through the spawning channel originates from Tom Browne Lake off the left fork. All the pinks born in this channel turn left into the relative safety of the deep holding pool. All the fish born further up the Glendale River system stay to the right fork and can travel another four or five miles if they need to.

The Glendale River Spawning Channel was built in the late 1980s by the D.F.O. It was built in response to rejuvenating a dead river. Over the previous couple of decades, the Glendale watershed had been devastated by massive clear cuts.

There were not enough trees left to hold the soil and debris on the mountain sides. Consequently, when it rained, torrents of water roared off the hills and carried wood, leaves, rocks and dirt down into the river. This effectively smothered the valuable gravel and natural habitat required for a healthy and viable fish population to survive.

There was no place left for the salmon to lay their eggs so this stock was virtually extinct. In order to repair the damage, a spawning channel was built. It is a continuous channel, about three kilometers long, weaving back and forth. It was dug out of a natural river flat and then a layer of ideal gravel was installed to the correct depth. Water was piped in from Tom Browne Lake, about a half a mile away, to provide the correct and adjustable flow of water to properly feed the new channel. The lake acts as a reservoir so a constant water volume is present year around.

The river, unlike the channel, is still subject to the whims of Mother Nature; high water levels after heavy rains or becoming almost dry when no rain falls for a while. The river's gravel bars can be moved by high river flows or left exposed during prolonged drought. The salmon seem to be able to withstand the vagaries of the natural river just fine. They have been surviving these natural occurrences for eons.

Once the salmon are in the holding pool at the spawning channel outlet, their trials are far from over. They may lay here for many days as their eggs ripen and bodies transform. When they are ready to go, they have another major obstacle to clear.

There is a dam to jump over. This dam regulates how deep the water is in the spawning grounds. Below the dam is a pool, in which the salmon can rest and get a running jump.

It is also here where the greatest numbers of grizzly bears patiently wait for their next meal. Here is where we see the greatest personal space tolerance amongst bears of all sizes. A well established pecking order is constantly evaluated, and may change in a moment by the arrival of a different bear. The jockeying for position in this fishing hole is continuous, as each day progresses and as each bear arrives or departs. There is surprisingly little conflict. Most of the time one of the bears just backs off a few feet, which seems to satisfy the other. Body language is the main tool used in this pool. All the bears recognize who is the dominant animal, and back off. Sometimes, especially young bears can't leave fast enough. The three and four year old youngsters, who still have little status in the bear world, just give way to every other bear. They don't want to get hurt arguing a fight they know they can't win. It is just much safer for them to go to another fishing hole that is not so crowded.

WHERE THE GREATEST NUMBERS OF GRIZZLY BEARS PATIENTLY WAIT...

I have seen these younger bears come marching down the trail with expectations of a bountiful fish dinner. Fueled by the wonderfully sweet odors of rotting salmon, not dissimilar to the reaction of the smell of a roasting turkey in our home, these youngsters suddenly skid to a halt when they break over the banks of the river only to see a dozen larger bears occupying the pool full of their salmon dinner. These juveniles cautiously turn around, hoping nobody noticed their indiscretion, and wander off toward a safer fishing hole. Occasionally, they will sit down in a safe position and wait their turn at the salmon smorgasbord.

SOOOFULL

I cannot eat another bite. It hurts!! Maybe a few eggs in a little while. Later in the season these bears become fussy about what they eat. In order to max out the calories per bite they will often discard the male salmon for a female. Even then the bears just eat the eggs, brains and skin. They discard the rest of the carcass for the benefit of the river, birds and scavenging bears.

One sow with three two year old cubs, we called 'the Gang', was particularly aggressive. When this gang emerged from the forest, she barely paused as she strode down to the weir. Almost all of the other bears made way, and if it wasn't quickly enough, she would hustle them on their way. She had a couple of favorite fishing holes and she demanded them. Whoever was the hapless victim in the wrong place at the wrong time was dealt with. Very little discussion was required.

Even one of her cubs was developing her attitude, as long as her mom was nearby. This cub would put the run on some bears, or slowly crowd out others. I wonder how she will make out next year when she doesn't have mom's backing. I do believe she is learning valuable lessons if she survives to become a mother herself someday. If you consider that the odds are fifty percent against all three bear cubs surviving the first year and a further twenty five percent against surviving subsequent years, a strong aggressive mother is obviously very beneficial to the well being of the grizzly bear species.

I was very impressed by the way this sow dealt with perceived problems. She got right with the program; no waffling, no delays, get it solved now, and get over it. She seemed to hold no grudges with other bears or her own cubs. If discipline was required it was handed out with the greatest dispatch and strength needed. One minute she could box her cub's ears and be playing in the pool with them the next.

I watched one day as The Gang was walking down a gravel bar beside the river. Out of the forest, minding his own business about fifty meters away, stepped a large male, going fishing. The gang matriarch ran directly toward this surprised boar. They were nose to nose, mouths agape, bellowing at each other. Their ears were laid back, their lips snarling, while balancing half erect on rear feet, front paws poised ready to do severe damage.

They did not touch each other but you can be sure they could taste their breath. The rest of the gang and the surrounding world stood still for thirty seconds as this drama took over.

Even the birds seemed to stop in mid flight expectantly waiting to see the outcome of this challenge. Slowly, not wanting to appear to be backing down, each combatant settled back onto three feet, one paw still poised. Hissing and chuffing and moaning ensued as each bear backed off a bit more. Heads were lowered in submission, angled sideways, eyes averted as to not challenge the other bear. The sow stood her ground as the male slowly backed up, severely chastised for his indiscretion. He seemed to know that it was not worth the risk of a severe wound for a fight that would gain neither combatant any benefit. At a different time of year or a different bear there would have been fur and blood flying, but the stakes would have been much higher. Today, however, he decided it best to go around and to pay a little more attention to who is in the neighborhood. The Gang gathered together back on their way up the river, the birds continued their flights and the community continued its daily struggles for survival.

THEY COULD TASTE THEIR BREATH

SHE DID NOT LIKE TO GET HER FEET WET

There was another mother who had one cub of the year who we named Princess. This cub was a delicate little female who seemed to need extra coaxing by a very patient and tolerant mother. She did not like to get her feet wet, was downtrodden by the rain and somewhat finicky with the fish her mother presented. Her hair stood on end after a swim, food stuck to her face while she ate and leaves clung to her coat as she followed her mom from the forest. Princess braved the rushing waters of the river but only with gentle encouragement under the watchful eye of her indulgent parent. The young royal would slowly walk through the cold fishy water to her favorite throne, a flat rock in the middle of the river, just below the weir, from which she could survey all the activity happening around her. When mom caught a fish, she would leave her perch and delicately tiptoe over to inspect the catch. If she deemed it worthy, she would take it from mom and gently nibble at her meal until losing it in the current, to be claimed by the shrieking gulls.

AS HER HIGHNESS HIGHNESS SAT ON HER THRONE

As her highness sat on her throne she was oblivious to the fish struggling in the shallows around her. She balefully watched the other bears, making sure nobody came too near. Mom also protectively watched her darling. Like all busy mothers, she did all she could for her child. She never got cross and dealt very gently, firmly and consistently with her delicate daughter. This pair was the last bears I saw that season. Long after all the other bears had left the spawning channel, I saw Mom and Princess trying to put on the last few pounds needed for the coming hibernation. All that was left for them to eat was the rotting fish carcasses on the river bottom and the eggs that they could sniff out on the exposed gravel bars. I look forward to their return next fall.

Some of the most amusing bears to watch are the sub-adults, the teenagers of the bear world. These are three to about five year olds, with lots to learn and dangers at every turn. We saw a set of twins, a boy and girl, come out of hibernation with their mother in the early spring.

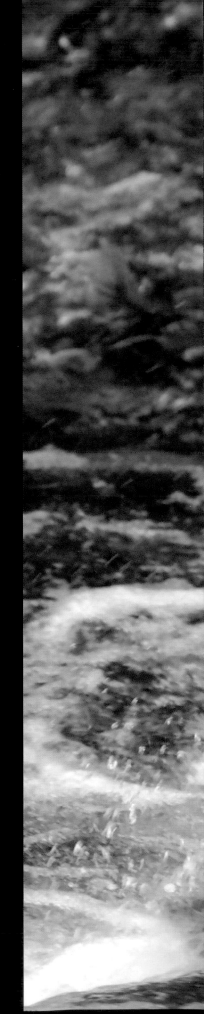

They hung out for about three or four weeks as a family group. Mom seemed to get them down to the estuary, made sure they knew where they were, and then left them. She found a mate, was bred, and then left the estuary soon after. The cubs stayed around until late summer and left also. These two kids were the background entertainment of the summer. They had so much to learn even though they had had a good education; however an education is not always the same as real experience. Now the siblings had to protect themselves and they did that by running. They were very alert as to who was around them. Any noise in the forest was enough reason for them to run at least a quarter of a mile before taking a look back. If any other bear could be seen, that was also excuse enough to run. The scent of a bear sent the twins on a gallop across the mudflats, water splashing, mud squirting and gulls scattering. A deer even scared them from their siesta on the beach one warm sunny afternoon. They were so busy running and watching to see who was about to hurt them that they almost ran another bear over. They had to run back the other way because they didn't know who was back there and who scared them in the first place, but they could see this bear. We always knew that if we saw the twins running, we could look back along their wake to see another bear or a deer step out of the forest fringe.

Usually we could find these two grazing on the sedges beside the estuary or the river delta. Out here in the open they felt secure. They could see a long distance, food was handy, and the river was close enough to have a dip in if it was too hot. Rocks on the beach were easy to roll over for crabs giving them some much needed protein and a break from all that salad. The forest was nearby to hide in, to get some shade or to pick berries. The brother was the leader; he was a little braver and always leading on the trail. He was a fun loving boy, where as his sister seemed a bit more serious. We never saw one without the other shadowing. One idyllic afternoon a group of us sat quietly across the river from these twins as they had a snooze on the edge of the grassy island. No wind ruffled the waters and a pair of kingfishers flew to and fro, busily trying to feed their hungry brood. Brother bear stood up, stretched like a big dog, and took a mouthful of sedge. As he calmly chewed he looked around for any demons. Sister bear raised her head, wondered what we were looking at, and then joined her brother. Out of curiosity brother stepped down off the bank and nonchalantly swam straight toward us. Not wanting to be left alone, sister joined him. We all sat there, quietly wondering what was on their mind.

They dog paddled slowly in our direction, and then adjusted their course so they could take a good look at each occupant of the boat as they swam alongside, only six feet away. Not really looking at us directly but watching out of the corner of their innocent brown eyes, nostrils cocked to our side, they slowly passed us by. Crawling up the bank of the river into the grass, they both paused, and glanced back at us in greeting. Giving a mighty shake, water droplets scattering everywhere, sparkling in the sun, the two cubs started grazing as if to say,' I guess you people are ok'.

Another young bear who hung around all summer was a male we called 'Seedy'. This bear was a troubled young boar, and not to be trusted. He ran the twins ragged every chance he got. Whenever he saw them, away he would go, trying to assert his dominance. He had obviously been abused in the past. He was scratched and scarred from past battles.

Even though he was a year older than the twins he was still a worried bear. The older, bigger bears had little tolerance for Seedy so they also chased and threatened him whenever he came too near. He was a darker color and not blonde like the twins. He was scrawny and poorly kept, and this added to his unsavory looks. No wonder he had such a chip on his shoulder. One day, just as I lowered the ramp off the herring skiff in preparation to unload my guests for a land tour looking at bear sign, I heard a gasp from the boat full of people. Here came the twins at a dead run around the point a few yards away. Surprised, as we were, the twins paused for half a second in mid stride, then kept coming. They cleared my ramp as I stood on the bow of the boat. Hot on their heels came Seedy, also surprised but still keeping up the chase. We watched as the three bears ran down the beach for a couple of minutes and then ran into the forest. I often wondered since then what would have happened if the bears had showed up fifteen seconds later when all the people on the boat would have been coming down the ramp. Timing is everything in this world. We did not have to walk far to look for bear tracks.

I GUESS YOU PEOPLE ARE OK

A couple hours later we saw all three bears along the beach and wondered what dynamics were going on here. Seedy hung around until August and disappeared. I think I saw him later in the season, strolling the beach, and unable to eat. This bear had a damaged lower jaw. It hung open with a large pocket of infection hanging underneath. I watched as he tried unsuccessfully to slurp a dead salmon carcass. He was still skinny and it was getting late in the season. I wish to see him again but have little hope.

During the salmon migration we had quite a few juvenile bears. A brother-sister set of twins spent most of the fall fishing where they could, between all the other bears. These two seemed to get along very well. They were watchful, careful, respectful and bold enough to be around so many other bears. They moved when they had to but just far enough to be of no threat to anybody. They seemed to be happy enough at the fringes of the pools, and were productive enough to steadily gain weight as the season progressed. These twins were happy-go-lucky pair who really enjoyed life.

They would spend a large part of the day just swimming and playing in the large pool below the weir. They were both blondes, with light colored bushy hairdos. They were busybodies, and always in a hurry to get to the fishing hole. They would splash right into the water, start fishing, eat a couple of salmon, then, full again, begin a game of wrestling. The brother was the instigator of the match, and often had to be told when sister had enough. She would try to ignore him, but a three hundred pound bear jumping on your back is difficult to dismiss. To indulge his desire to play, she would grab him in a playful bear hug, nip his ear and the match would be on again. Occasionally another single bear would join them. They would meet on a gravel bar and cautiously check each other out. I think these twins were about four years old and the other bear one year older. He was perhaps an only surviving cub. He was a bit larger, but really seemed to crave companionship.

SOME
BEARS
NOBODY
FOOLED
AROUND
WITH

He was always respectful and careful when playing with the
twins. Often he would just hang around with them as they went about the business of the day.
Another set of triplets were also fishing on the Glendale that fall. They were around four years old, and a
close family unit. They were like a train wherever they went, with one on the heels of the next. They rested
in a large heap as if to stay warm or for the comfort of safe companionship. This trio fished more often in
the river than the spawning channel, preferring less competition. They would be interested observers above
the weir as if bear watching at the grocery store. Once tired of that sport, as one, they would get up and
wander off up river back to the peace and quiet of their own home.

The reaction of the sub-adults when other bears appeared was often comedic. Some couldn't get away
quick or far enough. They would splash across the river, climb up the bank and run down the trail before
looking back to see if it was safe. Some of the young bears would slowly paddle to the other end of the
pool, giving the larger bears lots of respect.
Every bear seemed to know the others or were able to discern, via body language, their intentions. Some
bears nobody fooled around with. The mom with the triplets and mom with Princess were not to be trifled
with. They tolerated no disrespect from anyone. Only the very largest bears held their ground if they were
there first. The large male bears were also to be respected. They were very quiet but deliberate in their
movements. They moved slowly, giving everybody time to move. The boars wanted to fish in peace but on
their own terms, which most of the time they did.

PATCHES WAS
NOT A THREAT
TO ANYBODY

A few single females were also fishing here that fall. A bear we named Patches was a regular. She fished in the middle and lower reaches of the weir pool. Patches was not a threat to anybody so she was tolerated by the two moms. They would crowd her off if she got too close but Patches seemed comfortable around most of the bears. Patches had a multi-colored coat, which was very recognizable when we saw her coming. A medium size and build gave her the agility to be a good fisher. She did not waste too much effort or fumble around when catching fish. It seemed to me that Patches was expanding on her good basic training from her mom and was now ready to aid the next generation on her own. I hope to see her with a cub of her own next year.

Several other single females fished on the river and weir. Most went about their fishing very quietly and efficiently. Whether fishing or slurping eggs off the bottom, the females were only interested in gaining enough weight to hibernate comfortably. I'm sure many of them had mated and were potentially pregnant, so having a heavy fat body was top priority for them. Don't forget, the female bears may have mated last spring, but they are not pregnant. If they did mate, they are carrying a fertilized egg called a Blastocyst. If the females are carrying enough body fat by late October, this Blastocyst will attach itself to the uterus at which time the female will be officially pregnant. Since the bears don't eat once they hibernate, think how much stored energy is used up keeping mom alive. She also incubates up to three or four babies and then nurses them well enough and long enough to raise their birth weight from about one pound to around fifteen pounds. Her body will lose about one third of her weight through this process. The mother's milk is very rich so the young bear cubs grow very quickly while they nurse. I think some human mothers would not mind this style of pregnancy. Get pregnant, eat all you can, go to sleep, have a one pound baby, and wake up after six months, back to their svelte figure with a walking, talking and potty trained baby.

We had another female bear we called Hummer.
She would fish in the pools or at the weir, all the while moaning. The entire time she spent fishing a constant hum emanated from her. Nobody ever figured out why. She did not have any cubs so it was not a method of communication for her. None of the other bears seemed to mind her noise.

There were a few other females with babies, but they did not stay around the weir. Once there was the very rare sight; a sow with four cubs born this year. I did not personally see them but they were reported often enough. Photos were taken but my timing was off. Another female had triplets and another had twins. I was able to see these families. I expect there was just too much competition around the spawning channel fishing holes for these families to feel secure and seeing them was an exceptional event.

At times we would see five or six female bears fishing quietly around the spawning channel. Most of the time, they would pick a favorite spot. Here they would catch a few fish or slurp some eggs off the bottom. They were not pushovers or to be trifled with. Any other bears crowding them were dealt with once their personal line was crossed.

Do not confuse their quiet confidence with weakness.
Once stuffed, the female bears would quietly wander into the forest for a short nap before returning a couple of hours later.

THEIR SWEET SCENT RIDES THE INFLOW BREEZES

My favorite and I think the most dramatic bears to watch are the large boars. When one of these boars steps out of the forest, everybody notices. The air is charged with anticipation. Is he here to fish or to cause widespread mayhem? We all wait with baited breath, wondering what his mood is now. This mood changes with the season. We first see these dominant boars once spring has fully arrived. The estuary sedges are full green, and flush with new tender growth. This brings them down to the shore line.

Flowers have been blooming for a couple of weeks already. Their sweet scent rides the inflow breezes, inviting the hummingbirds and bees to spread their sweet nectars, fertilizing the berry bushes in the forest and the rice root on the sedge flats. The world around us is a hub-bub of activity. The birds, having selected their mates, are incubating their clutches of eggs.

The mother bears and older cubs have been here for a month already. Mom seems restless and her cubs don't understand why. She has brought them down to this same spot each of the three springs they've been alive.

IT IS TIME FOR YOU TO GO

Something is different this year. Mom spends more time tasting the wind and the trails they follow. Each of the rub trees gets more attention than normal. The cubs can smell it too. Strong odors of female and male bears mix with the smell of budding flowers and leaves. Mom is restless, and the cubs are nervous. One day in early June, if bears could talk like humans, I can hear mom say to her cubs, 'Kids, I've taught you all you need to know to survive in this dangerous world. It is time for you to go make your own way. You have each other for company and I have to go. This is the way of the bears. If we are to survive as bears, I have to start a new family. In a couple of years you will also start new bear families. It is very dangerous for you to be with me when I meet with the large males. Just remember all the spots I showed you where to find food, where to look for a den, and how to watch out for people and other bears. Good luck kids!' With that mom leaves her cubs grazing on the estuary as another instinct propels her to the forest marking tree. Within a few days she is met by a large male bear.

Late spring is the time of year that we as tourists and observers see these battle-scarred warriors of the forest. The males have already been fighting for the right to breed any of the sows in estrus. The males run themselves ragged trying to keep up to the females who are close to breeding time. Other male bears are also nearby so each bear has to watch out for their challenges. Many of these male bears are very shy of people. They are torn between the females grazing on the wide open estuary where people are watching from boats, or to the safety of the dense forest. We watched one large male that first spring who we called Bruno. He was almost twice as big as the females, and dark brown. His belly almost dragged on the ground as he tirelessly pursued these fickle females. He would stay on the trails, safely hidden just inside the forest edge. From here he could watch for intruders while at the same time guard his mate. If she wandered too far from him he would come charging out on to the beach in hot pursuit.

I would not like to be between Bruno and his mate at that time. Occasionally we would hear a grunt or cough of displeasure or warning from Bruno if someone came within his personal space. We did not see him fight and he did not appear with any fresh wounds or scars that spring. I like to think the bears treated him with as much respect as we humans tried to. We did not see Bruno around after the first of July but he surely did leave an impression with us.

BRUNO

The next male bears we saw showed up with the salmon. We would catch a fleeting glimpse of a wary bear, unused to our intrusion within his safety zone. As the days passed they would become more accustomed to our presence and routines.

The bears would acknowledge our visit with a baleful glance, then, and sensing nothing to fear, carry on with their day. I often wondered if the bears have a sense of our intentions by our approach and body language. Most of the time we first saw these bears fishing in the river. The dominant bears, of course, got the best fishing holes. The younger bears chased fish with one eye as the second eye watched for other bears.

LET THE FEAST
BEGIN

As more salmon returned from their journey to sea back to the Glendale, more bears began to dot the landscape. They began to move from the berry patches, and scavenged along the beaches of the cove and estuary toward the mouth of the river. Here at low tide was the first opportunity for the bears to catch their first sample of the fat juicy salmon this season. Let the feast begin. The younger male bears showed up first, competing with the females who had been here all summer. Soon most of these girls left for other fishing streams only to be replaced by new females and the male bears. As more fish began to fill the quiet pools along the river, the bear population began to grow. The first fish showed up at the beginning of August. The bear numbers grew steadily through September but were almost all gone by the end of October.

As the season progressed we could see the male numbers increase steadily. The older bears would approach from the dark safety of the forest on an obscure trail to suddenly appear at the bank of the river. The large male would slowly make his way to the fishing hole he had selected as the bear crowd watched. If his hole was occupied that occupying bear would slowly back off. Neither bear would make eye contact with the other. Very few challenges happened. If there was a confrontation, it was brief and no damage was done. The dominant females with cubs would often hold their ground against most bears but there were a few large males that no one challenged. Some of these bears bore their scars as badges of honor, earned on the battlefield over many campaigns. Some had chunks of hair missing, scars along their noses and ears missing. One had no claws on one foot and walked with a limp.

VAN GOGH

Van Gogh was another dominant bear who spent most of the autumn season fishing the Glendale. He was a very large bear who had one ear missing. I would hate to see the other guy after that fight. He was a dark chocolate brown color, with large head and feet. As the season progressed he grew even larger and more intimidating. Every other bear paid attention to what Van Gogh had in mind. He was only interested in eating all the fish he could. He was aware of how long the winters could be up here and was going to be well prepared.

One old boar was skinny, shabby and mostly toothless. The only teeth left were his front two canines which were worn down to one half their original lengths. His claws were long and sharp, his eyes bloodshot and his crooked nose added to his unsavory appearance. This bear was obviously very old but very tough. All other bears left him alone. He wasted no time nor energy when fishing, he was all business. He shared his hard won meal with no other bears and wasted little energy chasing off the scavenging birds. The crows and gulls were this old warrior's only companions. I hope to see him next year.

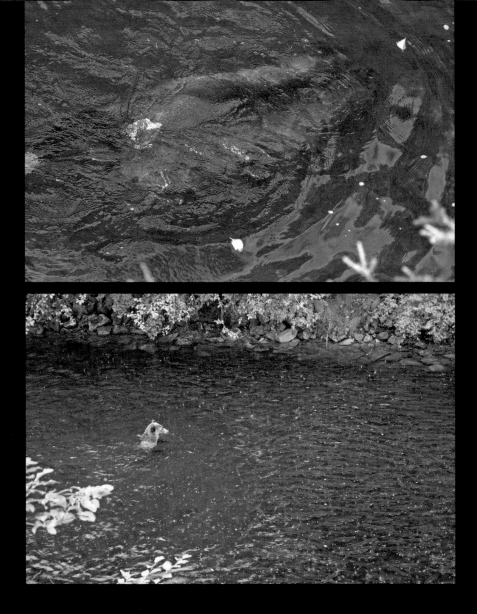

Another male bear who hung around the spawning
channel was a bear we called the Diver. This bear would spend most of
his time in the deeper pools completely submerged. He swam around the
pool looking for dead salmon carcasses which he brought to the surface
to check out. If he deemed them palatable they were eaten, but if not they
were discarded. The Diver spent hours floating effortlessly through the
pools full of ripening pink salmon. The bottom of the pool was littered
by the rotting fish he sorted through. I don't know what made one rotten
fish better tasting than another, but the Diver knew. It looked like he was
swimming in a large bowl of fish soup. The waiting salmon would leave a
clear ring around Diver as he swam. He did not waste any energy trying
to catch these live fish.

THE DARK AND DREARY FOREST

A very large brown bear also liked to fish the pool in front of the finger, where the spawning channel met the river The methodology he used was to stand on his back feet, concentrating on the bottom of the pool; he would then feel for a carcass. This morsel he would pass to a front paw and then to his big nose. If it passed the sniff test, he gently carried it to the far bank, settled his bulk down, half in the water, where he would dine in private comfort. No part of his fish was wasted. Once he cleaned up, he swam back into the pool for another tasty salmon.

I saw another old male bear one morning beside the tree stand in the river. It was one of those cold, wet mornings, with the rain tinkling onto the river surface in a steady drizzle. The old man's beard lichens hung from the alders and old Sitka spruce, giving a more eerie atmosphere to the dark and dreary forest.

The ravens and eagles were still on their roosts as our group of people waded into the river, unsure if we should have stayed in our beds. No sun filtered down this morning as we wait for who knows what to appear. An hour passed slowly as the damp chill seeped into our motionless bodies. Only the sound of the rain and the odd salmon making its way through the shallow riffle just below us reminded us that we were alive and attuned with Mother Nature. I was about to call off our tour early, thinking about hot coffee and a warm fire, when a movement in the river above us caught my eye. Out of the dark shadows in the river came a shape, and a large nose pushed a vee of water downstream to the pool at our feet.

Moss and Lichen

A VERY LARGE SCARRED UP BEAR

From the safety of our perch in the tree, cameras started clicking as a very large scarred up bear started to fish a few feet away. The cold and rain was forgotten as we admired the efficiency with which this boar caught fish. He fished the deeper pool, coming up with both live and dead fish. He ate what he caught. He swam over to a large submerged rock and sat on it in the middle of the stream. He shook the water from his ears, paused for a look, and then went back into the frigid river. He glanced up at us as he swam past as if to acknowledge our presence and crossed the river to the path we must take in a few moments to our waiting bus. I watched to see where he went but lost sight of him in the forest. He could take two different trails from there or break his own. I saw him as he headed up the hill from the bus stop but didn't say anything.

'Time to go' I called. Nobody wanted to go first, knowing where we had to go, but we were forced to by the soon to arrive float plane these folks had to catch. All senses were finely attuned as we crossed the river in that bear's wake. These guests will go home with that memory etched into the photo album in their brain. Rare encounters with notable animals of any kind leave impressions lasting a lifetime. When we are sitting around telling life's stories over the next many years, tales of these experiences will be told and retold to whoever will listen. Sometimes, the bears get bigger with more teeth and longer claws, or the wolves were closer, their howls were louder and the night was darker. We can never photograph some of these fleeting moments of time as well as our memories can. We remember the silence, the rain, the light, the chill of the air and the smell of rotting fish. We will recall the grizzly's glance, the way he swam and the way he disappeared into the forest beside our ride.

we will remember the anticipation we felt as we followed in his wake and looked at his footprints pressed into the mud on the trail. Rarely will our senses be so attuned to the forest around us. Right now a squirrel could send our heart to palpitations with a sudden scolding. Years from now, when we most need a break, we can be suddenly reminded of this time by the smell of fish, a dark rainy morning, or while rushing to catch a last minute flight. Memories of these times can make us pause for a moment during hectic days and take us back to a moment in time where we were at our best.

Whether we watched the wildlife from the viewing stands, tree stand or the boats, we have been privileged to meet these creatures on their own turf. The wonder of the salmon migration, the varied bird life, and the great grizzly bear have all helped us to understand how enduring this rugged landscape is, despite our worst efforts. They all need our help and support to survive our continued assault.

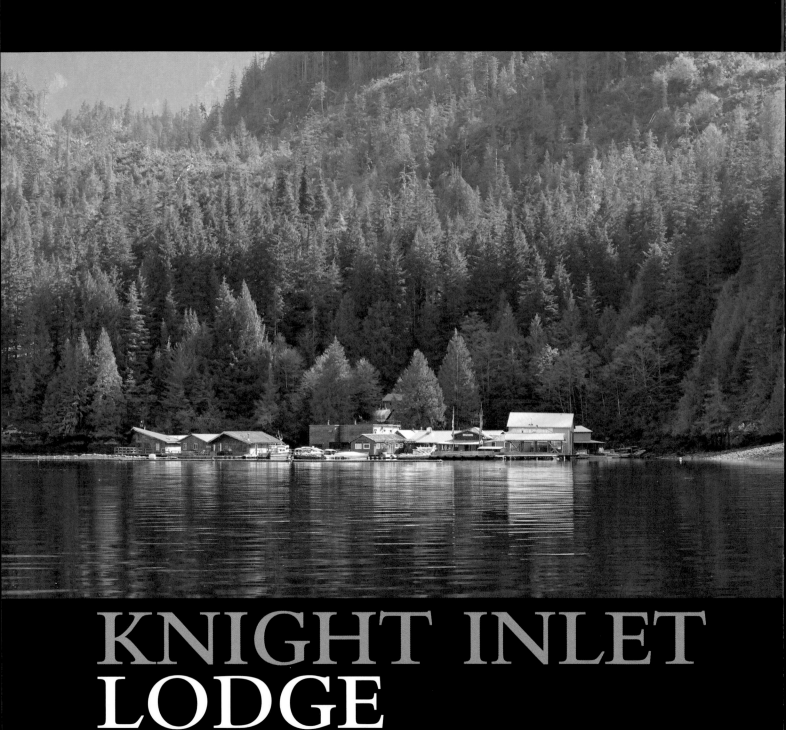

KNIGHT INLET
LODGE

Knight Inlet Lodge was moved to Glendale Cove in 1979 from Hoeya Sound where it had a long and glorious history as a 'men's only' fishing lodge. Fishing for the giant Chinook and Coho salmon was some of the best on the west coast of British Columbia. This tradition continued in Glendale Cove until 1996 when the present owners Dean and Kathy Wyatt bought and converted it to an eco, family friendly wildlife viewing destination. Since then it has become one of B.C.'s premier resorts entertaining guests from around the world. The main attraction is now the coastal grizzly bear, black bears, eagles and the annual pink salmon run. There are of course many other birds and wildlife to see along with whale watching tours, rainforest walks and boat trips to see the magnificent scenery of Knight Inlet. First class food and lodging along with the friendly and knowledgeable guides and support staff help make the guest's tours a trip of a lifetime.

Visit www.grizzlytours.com

When we use our valuable recourses such as the salmon or grizzly bears for our enjoyment and profit, I believe it is our duty to give something back to them. I have picked two organizations to help by donating a share of the proceeds of the sale of this book.

Vital Ground is the name of the first non-profit organization I chose because their mission is to protect and restore North American grizzly bear populations by conserving wildlife habitat. Vital Ground's motto is, 'Where the grizzly can roam, the earth is healthy and whole!' This means that while conserving habitat for the grizzlies, we are also helping out all the other plants and critters living in these wilderness areas. Because the range of the grizzly is so diverse, from the shores of the ocean and rivers through the forest to the high mountain meadows, saving grizzly range and habitat also benefits the entire plant and animal community.

Vital Ground was founded in 1990 by Doug and Lynne Seus, the owners and trainers of Bart the Bear. Bart, an Alaskan brown bear, is the animal star of several feature films, television movies and documentaries, including Legends of the Fall and The Bear. Through intelligence and loyalty, Bart was able to assist the delivery of a powerful message to mankind: 'clean up your act and learn from past mistakes.' Born in 1977 at a US zoo, Bart lived till May of 2000.

He grew from five pounds to fifteen hundred pounds of enthusiastic showmanship. He travelled with his human family throughout North America as a 'spokes bear' and ambassador for Vital Ground. Today, Bart's legacy is carried forth by Doug and Lynne Seus and 'Tank the bear'. A pair of orphaned cubs named 'Bart' and 'Honey-Bump Bear' follow in Bart's giant footsteps as well to bring the wondrous spirit of the great bear into many lives and hearts.

Vital Ground is dedicated to reconnecting isolated fragments of wild lands important for grizzly recovery and bio-diversity. They are a land trust placing special emphasis on protecting specific key landscapes. Based in Missoula, Montana, headquarters are centrally located near prime grizzly country. Most of their work happens in Montana, Idaho, Wyoming, Alaska and British Columbia. To date, Vital Ground has helped protect and enhance over 466,000 acres of crucial grizzly habitat in these areas.

Vital Grounds ultimate goal is to connect fragmented grizzly populations and habitat in the lower 48 states to the more robust populations in British Columbia and Alberta. This continuous corridor of wildlands would assist and safeguard the Great Bear's ability to travel unimpeded from Yellowstone all the way to the Yukon, as it historically did. Only in this way can the genealogical diversity continue to provide healthy and generous populations of umbrella species like the grizzly bear. Countless other animals, plants, birds and fragile ecosystems will benefit as well.

VITAL GROUND

I believe the dedicated and hardworking professionals at Vital Ground are doing great work for a very noble cause. We will all benefit by the enhancement of our wildlands and wild life, especially the 'Great Bear.'

Visit the Vital Ground web-site: www.vitalground.org

The other organization I have chosen to support
is a local group of volunteers called

'OYSTER RIVER ENHANCEMENT SOCIETY.'

'Never doubt that a small group of thoughtful committed citizens can change the world. Indeed, it is the only thing that ever has'. The truth of this quote by Margaret Mead is aptly demonstrated year after year by the volunteers at O.R.E.S. Led by an able and knowledgeable manager and a board of directors, men, women and school children from all walks of life combine their varied skills to operate an enhancement fish hatchery, located half way between Campbell River and Courtenay on the Oyster River. The O.R.E.S. was formed in 1983 by a small group of concerned citizens in an attempt to revitalize the decimated Oyster River. Since then volunteer membership has grown to over three hundred enthusiastic members. Their mission is to enhance, restore and protect fish and wildlife habitat on the Oyster River.

T h e   O . R . E . S . operates a strategic enhancement hatchery, raising Pinks, Chum, Coho, and Chinook salmon, producing up to two and a half million fry annually.

Using a combination 'low tech' and 'state of the art' enhancement techniques, along with scrounged, donated and new equipment, the society has transformed a dead river into one of the most productive volunteer driven salmon producers on Vancouver Island.

With a budget of only thirty thousand dollars per year, the O.R.E.S. incubates 2.5 million salmon eggs per year. They have built numerous spawning, rearing and over wintering channels to provide ideal rearing habitat for the salmonids and trout fry and smolts. Along with improving the fish habitat, other wildlife enjoy the improvements to the river as well. Elk, bear and deer as well as numerous species of birds including Wood Ducks now call the Oyster River home.

Even with such a small budget, it is challenging to raise the money needed to keep operating. Money is raised through government grants, community support, donations, fund raising and membership fees.

The Oyster River Enhancement Society demonstrates a twenty five year success story which continues to benefit our community at large. The leadership is sound, the volunteers are dedicated and the river is improving.

T h e   O . R . E . S . is not just about hard work. It is about having fun, fellowship, fishing and feeling good about a job well done. Many of the members enjoy the fruits of their labor when the salmon return or the steelhead and cuttys start biting. All the hard work is worth it for one good strike on a fly or a spinner.

Visit: www.oysterriverenhancement.org

Thanks go to many different people of many varied vocations for helping me create this story. Having been raised on a small farm in northern Alberta in the 1950s and 1960s, I was never far from the local wildlife. I tramped the fields, forests and the rivers hunting the meat, fish and berries for our table. I helped trap the numerous fur bearers of the area to provide extra income for the farm. Throughout many of the years of my working life I worked as a logger and took my family on hunting, fishing and camping trips, always to the forests, rivers and lakes of my youth.

I have to thank my Dad for starting me down the wilderness path. Together we passed many happy hours hunting the Bad Heart river valley, the grain fields, and the forest of our home.

Thanks to all the guys I worked with in the bush as loggers, cruisers and saw millers. We worked hard, we learned by trial and error, and had a lot of fun. Somebody always looked out for us.

Thanks to old friends and family who don't always understand our motives, but who continue to support us over the miles via e-mail and phone calls and prayers.

Thanks to David Pinel, my patient Coastal Adventure Tourism teacher at North Island College. Dave dragged me kicking and scratching out of my shell opening my eyes and thoughts to new and wondrous vistas and philosophies on the west coast of British Columbia. There were many different teachers of that course who helped open my eyes to the exciting possibilities of the tourism industry of B.C.

One of the guest speakers at the C.A.T. program was Tim McGrady, an employee of Knight Inlet Lodge who came to talk to our class about an exciting career as a bear watching guide. I knew as Tim was talking that I had found my niche. I'd like to thank Dean and Kathy Wyatt, Harold Payne, Jamie Scarrow and the staff of the lodge for taking me in as an 'old guy' guide. Frank Petruzelka and the volunteers at the Oyster River Enhancement Society who show me what a bunch of geezers can do when they put their minds and bodies to work for the good of the salmon and the river's other wildlife. My classmates and work mates, whom I work, play, learn and laugh with, earn my respect every day for their hard work, safety and dedication to the guests, the bears and the well being of the Glendale environment. Thanks to Doug Fieldhouse for encouraging and editing this project. New friends and co-workers never replace old ones, but do open our minds and hearts to all kinds of possibilities. `

Thanks to our guests, who traveled so far to see our magnificent scenery, opening their hearts and wallets for the grizzly and black bears. Without you, none of this can take place. I find that no matter where in this world we come from, we all share the same stories, tragedies and triumphs.

This story is dedicated to the memories of good friends who passed tragically too soon. Bernie, Russ and Doug; suicide, cancer and motor vehicle accidents all too often remind us of our own mortality. We are not guaranteed our allotted three score and ten, and had better utilize each day to the max to make this fragile world a better place to live.

Thanks to the capable staff at Kask Graphics for their encouragement and design expertise.
www.kaskgraphics.com

Of course, none of this could take place without the blessings and encouragement of my best friend and wife, Fay. I've known her for fifty years and she has been my partner for thirty four of them. She has been the rock and the stability throughout the raising of our family, Michael, Trina and Russell, and the various wild schemes I've been able to come up with. Fay has patiently taken on the job of typing and formatting my story. Without her tireless tolerance and hard work on this story and in our lives together, I don't think any of this would have taken place so easily.

THANKS

ACKNOWLEDGEMENTS

Source of information

Thanks to Fisheries and Oceans Canada. Reproduced with the permission of Her Majesty the Queen in Right of Canada, 2008.
Visit www.pac.dfo-mpo.gc.ca

Thanks to Grant MacHutcheon and the B.C. Bear Viewing Association for the educational seminars and ongoing support. Visit www.bearviewing.ca

Thanks to the Oyster River Enhancement Society for the training and opportunities to help raise salmon and awareness to our visitors from afar.
Visit www.oysterriverenhancement.org

Thanks to Ruth Labarge, Ali Oop and the rest of her bear menagerie for educating and entertaining the public about bear safety through educational demonstrations at the Wildlife Park at Innisfail, Alberta.

Thanks to North Island College in Campbell River, British Columbia for their great Coastal Adventure Tourism course and knowledgeable instructors.
Visit www.nic.bc.ca